Mel Bay Presents Stefan Grossman's Guitar Workshop Audio Series

Bottleneck Blues Guitar

taught by Stefan Grossman

**This book contains
3 compact discs
(3 full hours of instruction)
featuring note-by-note,
phrase-by-phrase instruction.**

CONTENTS

1 2 3 4 5 6 7 8 9 0

Visit us on the Web at www.melbay.com Ñ E-mail us at email@melbay.com

EXPLANATION OF THE TAB SYSTEM

"…Learning from listening is unquestionably the best way, the only way that suits this kind of music. You are setting the notes down for a record of what happened, a record that can be studied, preserved and so on, a necessary and useful companion to the recordings of the actual sounds. I keep thinking of this as I transcribe; if you could do it, it would be good to have a legend across each page reading : 'Listen to the record if you want to learn the song.'"

Hally Wood (taken from the Publisher's Foreword to the *New Lost City Ramblers Songbook*.)

These words are most suitable for introducing the tablature system, for tablature is just a guide and should be used in conjunction with the recordings. Tablature is not like music notation, however the combination of tab and music in an arrangement forms a complete language. Used together with the original recordings they give a total picture of the music.

The tab system does not attempt to show rhythms or accents. These can be found on the music or heard in the recordings. Music notation tackles these articulations to a degree, but the overall sensations, the feel and the soul of music cannot be wholly captured on the written page. In the words of the great Sufi Hazrat Inayat Khan: "…The traditional ancient songs of India composed by great Masters have been handed down from father to son. The way music is taught is different from the Western way. It is not always written, but is taught by imitation. The teacher sings and the pupil imitates and the intricacies and subtleties are learned by imitation."

This is the theme I've tried to interpolate into the tablature. Tablature is the roadmap and you are the driver. Now to the tab:

Each space indicates a string. The top space represents the first string, second space the second string, etc. A zero means an open string, a number in the space indicates the fretted position, for instance a 1 in a space indicates the first fret of that string.

In the diagram below the zero is on the second string and indicates the open second string is played. The 1 is placed on the third string and signifies the first fret of the third string. Likewise, the 4 is in the fourth space and indicates the fourth fret of the fourth string.

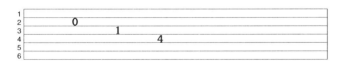

Generally for fingerpicking styles you will be playing the thumb, index and middle fingers of your picking hand. To indicate the picking finger in tab the stems go up and line up down from the numbers.

A. A stem down means that your thumb strikes the note.
B. If a stem is up, your index or middle finger strikes the note. The choice of finger is left up to you, as your fingers will dictate what is most comfortable, especially when playing a song up to tempo!

C. The diagram below shows an open sixth string played with the thumb followed by the second fret of the third string played with the index or middle finger:

In most cases the thumb will play an alternating bass pattern, usually on the bass strings. The index and middle fingers play melodic notes on the first, second and third strings. Please remember, this is not a rule; there are many exceptions.

In fingerpicking there are two "picking" styles: Regular picking and "pinching" two notes together. A pinch is shown in the tab by a line connecting two notes. A variation of this can also be two treble notes pinched with a bass note. Follow the examples below from left to right:

1) The open sixth string is played with the thumb.
2) The first fret of the sixth string is pinched together with the third fret on the third string. The sixth string is played with the thumb, the third string with the index finger.
3) The thumb strikes the third fret of the fourth string.
4) The first fret/sixth string is played with the thumb; it's pinched with two notes in the treble. The index and middle fingers strike the first fret/first string and the third fret/second string.
5) The next note is the index finger hitting the first fret/second string.
6) Lastly, the bass note is played with the thumb on the third fret/fourth string.

There are certain places in blues and contemporary guitar that call for the use of either strumming techniques or accented bass notes. The tab illustrates these as follows:

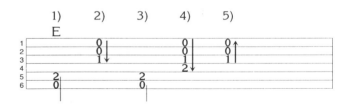

1) The thumb hits the open sixth string and the second fret on the fifth string should also sound. For example, play an E chord. Now strike the open string and vary the force of your attack. Try hitting it hard enough so that the fifth string vibrates as well. This technique is very important for developing a full sound and the right alternating bass sound.

2) Next the arrow notation indicates a brush and the arrowhead indicates the direction of the brush.

    A. If the arrowhead is pointed down, the hand brushes up towards the sixth string.
    B. If pointed up, the hand brushes down towards the first string.
    C. The number of strings to be played by the brush is shown by the length of the arrows. For example, this arrow shows a brush up toward the sixth string, but indicates to strike only the first, second and third strings.
    D. The brush can be done with your whole hand, index finger or middle and ring finger. Let comfort plus a full and "right" sound guide your choice.

3) The third set of notes again shows the sixth string/open bass note played with the thumb and being struck hard enough to make the fifth string/second fretted position sound.

4) Once more an arrow pointed downward indicates a brush up. This example forms an E chord and the brush up includes the first, second, third and fourth strings.

5) The last set of notes has an arrow pointed upward, indicating a brush downward striking the first, second, and third strings.

Here are several special effects that are also symbolized in tablature:

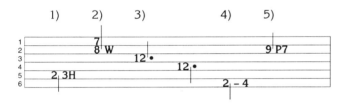

1) HAMMER-ON: Designated by an "H" which is placed after the stem on the fret to be hammered. In the example above, fret the second fret/fifth string and pick it with your thumb. Then "hammer-on" (hit hard) the third fret/fifth string, i.e. fret the third fret/fifth string. This is an all-in-one, continuous motion which will produce two notes rapidly with one picking finger strike.

2) WHAM: Designated by a "W." In the example the eighth fret/second string is "whammed" and played with the seventh fret/first string. Both notes are played together with your index and middle fingers respectively. The whammed note is "stretched." We do this by literally bending the note up. We can "wham" the note up a half tone, full tone, etc.

3) HARMONICS: Symbolized by a dot (•). To play a harmonic: gently lay your finger directly above the indicated fret (don't press down!) The two notes in the example are both harmonics. The first on the twelfth fret/third string is played with the index/middle finger, while the second note—twelfth fret/fourth string—is played with the thumb.

4) SLIDE: Shown with a dash (–). Play the second fret/sixth string and then slide up to the fourth fret of the sixth string. This is a continuous movement: the string is struck once with your thumb.

5) PULL-OFF: "P" designates a "pull-off." Fret both the seventh and ninth frets on the second string. Play the ninth fret with your index/middle finger and then quickly remove it in the same stroke, leaving the seventh fret/second string. Pull-offs are generally in a downward direction.

6) In certain cases other specific symbols are added to the tab, for instance:
    A. For ARTIFICIAL HARMONICS an "X" is placed after the fretted position.
    B. For SNAPPING a note an indication may be given with a symbol or the written word.

Many times these special techniques are combined, for instance putting a pull-off and a hammer-on together. Coordination of your fretting and picking hands will be complex initially, but the end results are exciting and fun to play.

PICKING HAND POSITION FOR FINGERPICKING STYLES: The Classical and Flamenco schools have strict right-hand rules, however for this style of acoustic fingerpicking there are NO RULES, only suggestions. Your right hand position should be dictated by comfort, however in observation of many well-known fingerpickers I found one hand position similarity—they all tend to rest their little finger and/or ring finger on the face of the guitar. This seems to help their balance for accenting notes and control of the guitar. Experiment with this position: it may feel uncomfortable at first. I ask my students to perfect this position and then compare the sound to when their finger(s) were not placed on the face of the guitar. They usually find the sound is greatly improved when some contact is kept with the guitar face.

MUSIC NOTATION: We have somewhat adapted the music notation in that this also shows whether the note is picked with your thumb or index/middle fingers. The stems of the music notes correspond to the direction of the tab stems. I hope this will make the music notation clearer to fingerpicking guitarists.

I hope you will feel at home and comfortable with the tablature and musical notations. Remember, these are only road maps indicating where and how you should place your fingers. The playing and musical interpretation is up to you.

BANTY ROOSTER

Trad.Arr. by Stefan Grossman ©2003 Shining Shadows Music All Rights Reserved. Used by Permission.

Open G Tuning: DGDGBD

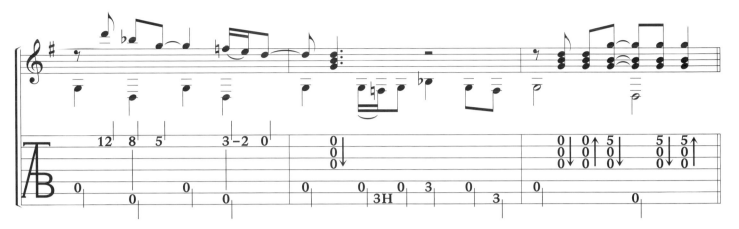

Son House

5

ONE KIND FAVOR

Trad.Arr. by Stefan Grossman ©2003 Shining Shadows Music All Rights Reserved. Used by Permission.

Open G Tuning: DGDGBD

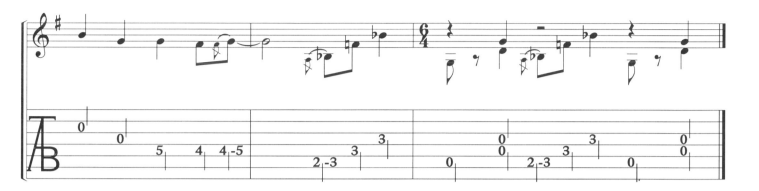

7

WAKE UP MAMA

Trad.Arr. by Stefan Grossman ©2003 Shining Shadows Music All Rights Reserved. Used by Permission.

Open D Tuning: DADF#AD

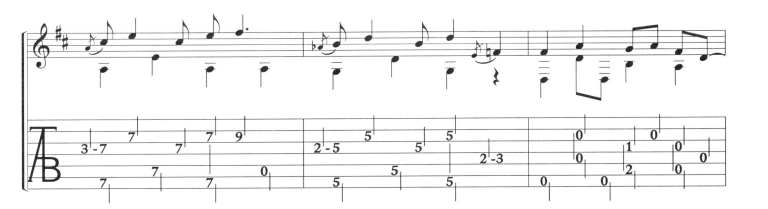

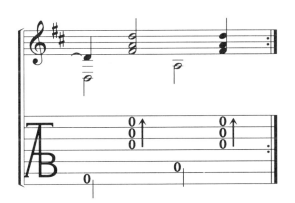

YOU GOT TO MOVE

By Fred McDowell & Rev. Gary Davis © Tradition Music (BMI) Administered by BUG & Chandos Music All Rights Reserved. Used by Permission.

Open D Tuning: DADF#AD

Swing Tempo

Fred McDowell

God Moves On The Water

Trad.Arr. by Stefan Grossman ©2003 Shining Shadows Music All Rights Reserved. Used by Permission.

Open D Tuning: DADF#AD

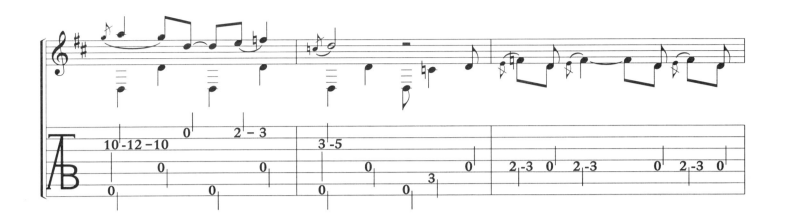

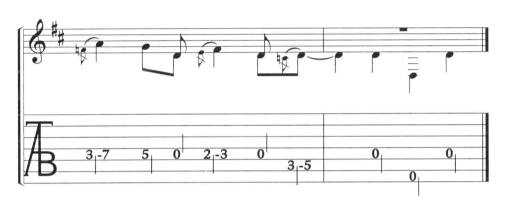

GOOD MORNING LITTLE SCHOOLGIRL

By Fred McDowell ©Tradition Music (BMI) Administered by BUG   All Rights Reserved. Used by Permission.

Open D Tuning: DADF#AD

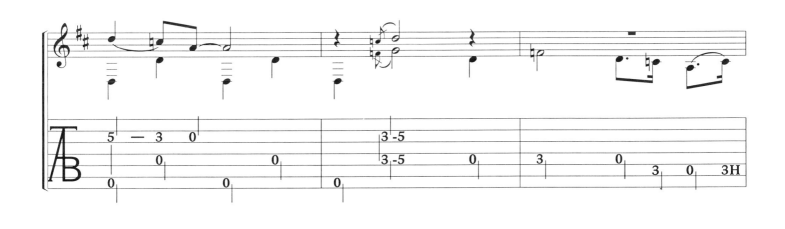

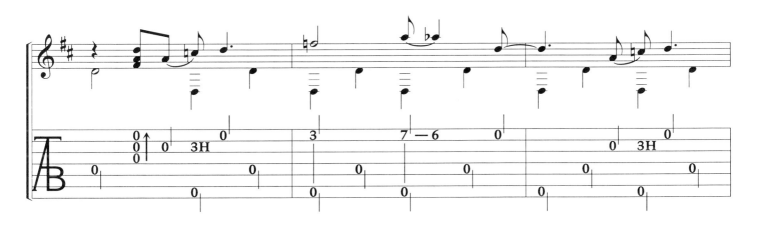

I Can't Be Satisfied

By McKinley Morganfield ©Watertoons Music (BMI) Administered by BUG All Rights Reserved. Used by Permission.

Open G Tuning: DGDGBD

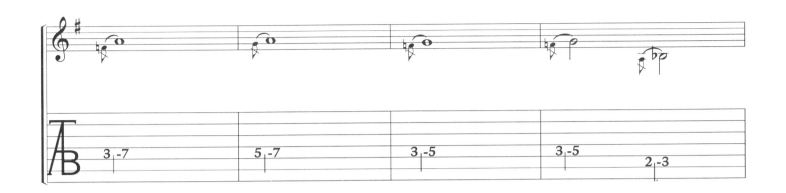

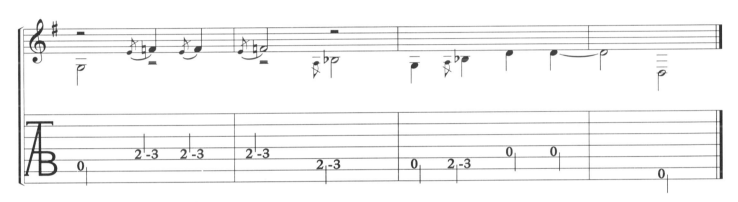

Muddy Waters

SOMEDAY BABY

Trad.Arr. by Stefan Grossman ©2003 Shining Shadows Music All Rights Reserved. Used by Permission.

Open G Tuning: DGDGBD

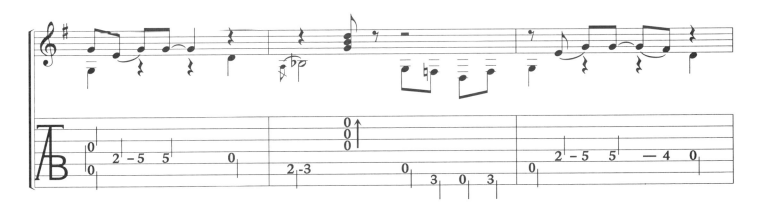

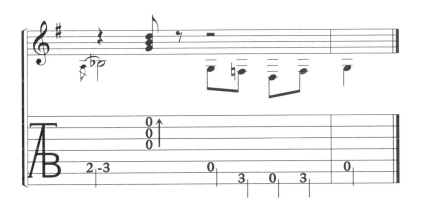

"Away Down South In Dixey" Chickamauga Park, GA   *a Keystone Stereo View Card*

ROLL AND TUMBLE BLUES

Open G Tuning: DGDGBD

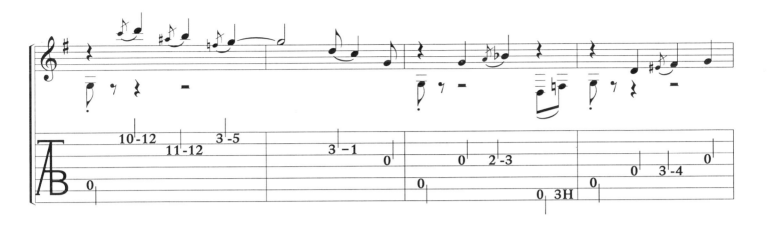

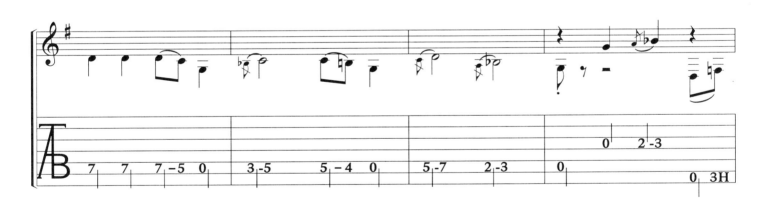

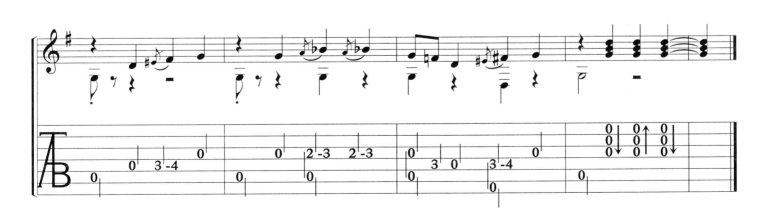

Delta Blues Guitar
Taught by Stefan Grossman

The Mississippi Delta of the 1920s-1940s was a treasure chest of powerful blues performances. For the intermediate guitarist. 16 page tab/music book with three compact discs.

LESSON ONE: Two famous Delta blues in the key of E. Willie Brown's *M&O Blues* and *Tommy Johnson's Bye Bye Blues.*

LESSON TWO: Willie Brown's *Future Blues* in an Open G tuning (D G D G B D) presents many of the hallmark licks that were also used by Willie's two close friends: Charlie Patton and Son House. Mississippi John Hurt played totally differently in the Open G tuning and we discuss his arrangement of *Frankie.*

LESSON THREE: Recorded in 1942 by Alan Lomas for the Library of Congress, Willie Brown's *Mississippi Blues* (a different Willie Brown then the one presented in our first two lessons) is an unusual Delta blues played in the key of A that imitates the popular piano blues of its time. This unusual arrangement has become a standard in todays fingerpicking repertoire. We conclude this lesson with a discussion of various blues licks in A. *GW99467 $24.95*

Ragtime Guitar
Taught by Stefan Grossman

This set of three lessons presents a variety of stringband rags to classic rags to novelty instrumentals. For the intermediate and advanced guitarist. 32 page tab/music book with three compact discs.

LESSON ONE: Two New Orleans standards are presented in this lesson. Both are played in the key of C with a style that combines an alternating bass with single-string runs and counterpoint lines. *Mabel's Dream* was popularized by the King Oliver Band. *High Society* is a well known Mardi Gras instrumental.

LESSON TWO: Two rags are presented in this lesson. We begin in a dropped D tuning with the classic rag *Powder Rag.* This is followed by an arrangement of the 1928 Dallas String Band recording of *Dallas Rag.* This combines alternating bass with counterpoint techniques and single-string runs.

LESSON THREE: One of Rev. Davis's most popular show instrumentals was *Soldier's March.* It has sections played in the keys of F and C and is a challenging guitar solo that takes the listener from early morning to lights out in the day of a soldier. *GW99459 $24.95*

Country Blues Guitar
in Open Tunings
Taught by Stefan Grossman

Open tunings have been used by many country blues guitarists. From the alternating bass styles of Furry Lewis and Mississippi John Hurt to the evocative and haunting sounds of Skip James to the ragtime blues of Blind Blake. In this series we discuss some of the finest guitar arrangements played in open tunings. For the intermediate guitarist. 32 page tab/music book with three compact discs.

LESSON ONE: OPEN G TUNING: Furry Lewis's *Turn Your Money Green* and Skip James's *Special Rider.*

LESSON TWO: OPEN D TUNING: *Vestapol*, Blind Blake's *Police Dog Blues* and Mississippi John Hurt's *If You Don't Want Me.*

LESSON THREE: OPEN D TUNING: Furry Lewis's *Kassie Jones*; Doc Watson's *Sitting On Top Of The World*; CROSSNOTE TUNING: Skip James's *Hard Time Killin' Floor* and *I'm So Glad.*
GW99466 $24.95

Country Blues Guitar
Taught by Stefan Grossman

Country Blues Guitar styles span a wide horizon. In these three lessons the ideas and techniques of Rev. Gary Davis, Charley Jordan, Tommy Johnson and Mississippi John Hurt are presented. The arrangements vary from alternating bass to a Delta strum to a monotonic bass. For the intermediate guitarist. 24 page tab/music book with three compact discs.

LESSON ONE: Rev. Davis's *Cocaine Blues* and *You Got The Pocket Book, I Got The Key* both played in the key of C and in what Rev. Davis called "old fashion' picking". The popular blues *Crow Jane* played in the key of E.

LESSON TWO: Charley Jordan's *Keep It Clean* and *Hunkie Tunkie Blues* both played in the key of E and presenting Jordan's unusual blues approach. Tommy Johnson's *Canned Heat* played in dropped D tuning.

LESSON THREE: We begin with *Come Back Baby*, a slow blues in A using a monotonic bass. We follow this with Mississippi John Hurt's *Monday Morning Blues* also played in the key of A but using an alternating bass. *GW99465 $24.95*

Fingerpicking Blues
Guitar Instrumentals
Taught by Stefan Grossman

A challenging set of three lessons featuring six blues instrumentals for the intermediate to advance guitarist. These guitar solos present a variety of techniques including counterpoint lines, rhythmic variations, blues vibrato and piano style arrangements. These are instrumentals I have recorded and performed in concert. 32 page tab/music book with three compact discs.

LESSON ONE: *Tribute To Lonnie Johnson*, a blues in the key of D played in a dropped D tuning (D A D G B E). *Dollartown*, combines a New Orleans sound with the playing of Rev.Gary Davis in the key of C.

LESSON TWO: *Yazoo Basin Boogie* played in a dropped D tuning (D A D G B E) combining a boogie, walking bass, counterpoint lines and Delta blues techniques. *Religious Trainfare Blues* (also titled *A Heart Much Obliged*) is played in the key of E and is reminiscent of the blues piano playing of Ray Charles.

LESSON THREE: *Blues For The Mann* is played in the key of A and features a multi-section piano sounding blues transcribed to fingerstyle guitar. *Lemon's Jump* is also played in the key of A and is influenced by the blues guitar of New Orleans great Snooks Eaglin. *GW99806 $24.95*

The Guitar Of Blind Blake
Taught by Woody Mann

Blind Blake was the premier ragtime blues guitarist of the 1920s. His fingerpicking techniques and styles are fascinating and challenging. He explored, extended and experimented with the alternating bass style that was popular at the turn of the century so that it could encompass the current trends in rhythmic dance beats and the more complex blues ideas coming from the emerging jazz bands. His guitar playing influenced generations of country blues artists. 24 page tab/music book with three compact discs.

TUNES PRESENTED INCLUDE: *Black Dog Blues, Bad Feeling Blues, Sweet Jivin' Mama, Diddie Wa Diddie and Blind Arthur's Breakdown.*

LESSON ONE: Blind Blake recorded many slow blues in the key of C. *Black Dog Blues* illustrates many of the licks and ideas that Blake used. *Bad Feeling Blues* is played in the key of D and presents a departure from Blake's usual phrasing patterns.

LESSON TWO: *Sweet Jivin' Mama* is a blues in A, played in a quasi-open D tuning (E A D F# A D)! This unusual arrangement brings together beautiful voicings with a lyrical blues setting. Blind Blake's most popular song for today's audience is *Diddie Wa Diddie*. This fast ragtime blues in C highlights Blake's thumb rolls.

LESSON THREE: *Blind Arthur's Breakdown* is a rag in the key of C that brings together a distinct five section instrumental combining thumb rolls, hot blues licks and unusual chord structures. This arrangement is a great challenge. *GW98507 $24.95*

The Guitar Of Big Bill Broonzy
Taught by Woody Mann

Big Bill Broonzy's recording career spanned the 1920s until his death in 1958. His repertoire was well recorded, from solo to duets to ensemble playing. He recorded for almost every Race label of the 1920s-1940s. He was rediscovered just as the "folk revival" was beginning in the mid-1950s and made a series of exciting albums for Folkways Records as well as recording various albums during European tours. He was a master of ragtime and country blues guitar. His playing was highlighted by a strong pulsating bass and melodic lead lines. It is a very powerful and challenging guitar style. In this series Woody Mann captures the essence of Big Bill's playing. 24 page tab/music book with three compact discs.

TUNES PRESENTED INCLUDE: *House Rent Stomp, Brownskin Shuffle, Moppin' Blues, Hey Hey, Worry You Off My Mind, Stovepipe Stomp and Saturday Night Rub.*

LESSON ONE: *House Rent Stomp* and *Brownskin Shuffle* are presented in this lesson. These two tunes illustrate Big Bill's playing of blues and rags in the Key of C.

LESSON TWO: This lesson presents three excellent examples of Big Bill's blues playing in the Key of A and E. His melodic lead lines played against a solid monotonic bass are illustrated with *Moppin' Blues, Hey Hey* and *Worrying You Off My Mind.*

LESSON THREE: To complete our study we look at his *Stovepipe Stomp* played in the Key of D and *Saturday Night Rub* played in the Key of G. *GW98508 $24.95*

The Guitar Of Lonnie Johnson
Taught By Woody Mann

Lonnie Johnson was the "governor" of blues guitar in the 1920's. His playing combined incredibly fast melodic runs with evocative blues licks. His playing was the forerunner of jazz and rock guitar. Lonnie Johnson's playing is highly challenging, provocative and exciting. His recordings from the 1920s were highly influential among all bluesmen and widely imitated. His incredible skill on the fingerboard also made him popular among jazz players. Lonnie recorded countless solo records as well as accompanying Texas Alexander, Louis Armstrong, Duke Ellington and Eddie Lang. 24 page tab/music book with three compact discs.

TUNES PRESENTED INCLUDE: *Away Down In The Alley, Woke Up This Morning With Blues In My Fingers, Go Back To Your No Good Man, Blues In G and Stompin' 'Em Along Slow.*

LESSON ONE: *Away Down In The Alley* is a blues guitar solo played in the key of D but with the guitar tuned D G D G B E. The playing combines blues left hand techniques with an intermittent fingerstyle approach. The end result is one of the most unique and powerful blues solos ever recorded.

LESSON TWO: *Woke Up This Morning With Blues In My Fingers* combines intriguing single–string blues runs with the use of diminished chords played in the key of D. This yields a unique blues guitar instrumental. *Go Back To Your No Good Man* is an example of how Lonnie accompanied a straight blues.

LESSON THREE: Lonnie Johnson played mostly in the key of D but he recorded one instrumental solo titled *Blues In G* which is presented in this lesson. This combines country blues licks with an uptown feel. We conclude the series with *Stompin' 'Em Along Slow* which is another killer blues instrumental in the key of D. *GW98509 $24.95*

The Early Roots Of Robert Johnson
Taught by Woody Mann

The music of Robert Johnson was greatly influenced by Son House, Skip James, Hambone Willie Newbern and Charlie Patton. Melodies and hot licks from the 1920s recordings of Scrapper Blackwell, Lonnie Johnson and Blind Blake can also be heard in Robert Johnson's recordings. In this three CD series, Woody Mann traces the development of Robert Johnson's music. 32 page tab/music book with three compact discs.

TUNES PRESENTED INCLUDE: *Kokomo Blues, Blue Day Blues, My Black Mama, Devil Got My Woman, Roll And Tumble, Screamin' And Hollerin', Georgia Bound and Lifesaver Blues.*

LESSON ONE: Scrapper Blackwell was a popular 1920s blues artist who recorded solo as well as countless sides with the great pianist, Leroy Carr. His unique rhythmic style and use of melodic treble licks can be heard in his *Kokomo Blues* (key of D) and *Blue Day Blues* (key of A). Robert Johnson freely adapted Scrapper's techniques to his playing.

LESSON TWO: Johnson was a teenager when he met and learned from Son House. Son's *My Black Mama* was copied by Johnson in his *Walkin' Blues*. Skip James's *Devil Got My Woman*, played in a crossnote tuning, was the basis for Johnson's *Hellhound On My Trail*. Blind Willie Newbern's *Roll And Tumble Blues* was the foundation for Johnson's *Traveling Riverside Blues*. Charlie Patton's *Screamin' And Hollerin'* played in an open G tuning, presents many licks and rhythmic ideas that Johnson used.

LESSON THREE: The recordings of Lonnie Johnson and Blind Blake influenced bluesmen from the East Coast to Texas to the Mississippi Delta. Blake's *Georgia Bound* presents an identical melody to Johnson's *From Four Until Late*. Lonnie Johnson's *Lifesaver Blues* presents hot licks and a melody used by Johnson. *GW98510 $24.95*

23

CD Track Listings

The audio lessons in this series were originally recorded in the 1970s. They were initially released on audio cassettes. We have gone back to our master tapes to get the best possible sound for this new CD edition. The complete contents of the original recordings have been maintained but certain references to albums that are no longer available or information that is out of date have been edited out .

These lessons originally came with different print material. These were handwritten and in some cases offered only tab transcriptions. The lessons have now been typeset in tab/music. As a result some spoken references on the CDs regarding page numbers or a position of a line or phrase on a page may differ slightly from the written tab/music in this new edition. We have annotated as carefully and exactly as possible what each track on the CDs present. Please use these track descriptions as your reference guide.

Lesson One

Track 1: Discussion on guitar setup for Bottleneck Blues
Track 2: Tuning to Open G tuning (D G D G B D)
Track 3: Discussion of bottleneck/slide techniques
Track 4: Performance of *Banty Rooster*
Track 5: Teaching of first phrase of *Banty Rooster*
Track 6: Plays first phrase of *Banty Rooster*
Track 7: Teaching of second phrase of *Banty Rooster*
Track 8: Plays first and second phrases of *Banty Rooster*
Track 9: Teaching of third and fourth phrases of *Banty Rooster*
Track 10: Plays first four phrases of *Banty Rooster*
Track 11: Teaching of last phrase of *Banty Rooster*
Track 12: Plays slowly *Banty Rooster*
Track 13: Introduces various recorded versions of *Banty Rooster*
Track 14: Performance from 1965 *How To Play Blues Guitar* of *Banty Rooster*
Track 15: Charlie Patton's recording of *Banty Rooster*
Track 16: Jo Ann Kelly and Stefan perform *One Kind Favor*
Track 17: Solo performance of *One Kind Favor*
Track 18: Teaching of first phrase of *One Kind Favor*
Track 19: Teaching of second phrase of *One Kind Favor*

Track 20: Plays first and second phrases of *One Kind Favor*
Track 21: Plays first and second phrases again of *One Kind Favor*
Track 22: Teaching of last phrase of *One Kind Favor*
Track 23: Plays *One Kind Favor*
Track 24: Blind Lemon Jefferson's recording of *One Kind Favor*
Track 25: Son House's recording of *Country Farm Blues*
Track 26: Tuning to Open D tuning (D A D F# A D)
Track 27: Discussion about chording with the bottleneck/slide
Track 28: Jo Ann Kelly and Stefan perform *Wake Up Mama*
Track 29: Solo performance of *Wake Up Mama*
Track 30: Teaching of first phrase of *Wake Up Mama*
Track 31: Teaching of second phrase (start of verse) of *Wake Up Mama*
Track 32: Plays verse until G chord of *Wake Up Mama*
Track 33: Plays verse again until G chord of *Wake Up Mama*
Track 34: Teaching from G chord of *Wake Up Mama*
Track 35: Plays *Wake Up Mama*
Track 36: Teaching of alternate lick of *Wake Up Mama*
Track 37: Blind Willie McTell's recording of *Mama T'ain't Long Fo' Day*
Track 38: Bo Weavil Jackson's recording of *You Can't Keep No Brown*

Lesson Two

Track 1: Fred McDowell performs *You Got To Move*
Track 2: Tuning to Open D tuning (D A D F# A D)
Track 3: Discussion on Fred McDowell's slide playing
Track 4: Plays *You Got To Move*
Track 5: Teaching of first phrase of *You Got To Move*
Track 6: Teaching of second phrase of *You Got To Move*
Track 7: Plays first and second phrases of *You Got To Move*
Track 8: Teaching of third phrase of *You Got To Move*
Track 9: Plays first three phrases of *You Got To Move*
Track 10: Teaching of fourth phrase of *You Got To Move*
Track 11: Teaching end phrase of *You Got To Move*
Track 12: Plays *You Got To Move*
Track 13: Introduction to Blind Willie Johnson's playing
Track 14: Blind Willie Johnson's recording of *God Moves On The Water*
Track 15: Plays *God Moves On The Water*
Track 16: Teaching of first phrase of verse of *God Moves On The Water*
Track 17: Teaching of second phrase of verse of *God Moves On The Water*
Track 18: Teaching of third phrase of verse of *God Moves On The Water*
Track 19: Plays first three phrases of verse of *God Moves On The Water*
Track 20: Teaching of fourth phrase of verse of *God Moves On The Water*
Track 21: Teaching of fifth phrase of verse of *God Moves On The Water*
Track 22: Plays verse of *God Moves On The Water*
Track 23: Teaching of first phrase of chorus of *God Moves On The Water*
Track 24: Plays first phrase of chorus of *God Moves On The Water*
Track 25: Teaching of second phrase of chorus of *God Moves On The Water*

Track 26: Plays first two phrases of chorus of *God Moves On The Water*
Track 27: Teaching of third phrase of chorus of *God Moves On The Water*
Track 28: Plays last third phrase of chorus of *God Moves On The Water*
Track 29: Plays slowly complete arrangement of *God Moves On The Water*
Track 30: Performance from 1965 *How To Play Blues Guitar* of
God Moves On The Water
Track 31: Memphis Minnie's recording of *Good Morning Little Schoolgirl*
Track 32: Jo Ann Kelly and Stefan perform *Good Morning Little Schoolgirl*
Track 33: Plays *Good Morning Little Schoolgirl*
Track 34: Teaching of first phrase of *Good Morning Little Schoolgirl*
Track 35: Teaching of second phrase of *Good Morning Little Schoolgirl*
Track 36: Plays first two phrases of *Good Morning Little Schoolgirl*
Track 37: Teaching of third phrase of *Good Morning Little Schoolgirl*
Track 38: Teaching of fourth phrase of *Good Morning Little Schoolgirl*
Track 39: Plays first four phrases of *Good Morning Little Schoolgirl*
Track 40: Teaching of fifth phrase of *Good Morning Little Schoolgirl*
Track 41: Plays first five phrases of *Good Morning Little Schoolgirl*
Track 42: Teaching last phrase of *Good Morning Little Schoolgirl*
Track 43: Plays slowly *Good Morning Little Schoolgirl*
Track 44: Plays up to tempo *Good Morning Little Schoolgirl*
Track 45: Plays *Good Morning Little Schoolgirl* leaving out some bass notes
Track 46: Fred McDowell plays of *Good Morning Little Schoolgirl*
Track 47: John Lee Hooker plays *Good Morning Little Schoolgirl*
Track 48: Teaching of various Fred McDowell licks

Lesson Three

Track 1: Introduction
Track 2: Muddy Water's recording of *I Can't Be Satisfied*
Track 3: Tuning to open G tuning (D G D G B D)
Track 4: Teaching of first and second phrases of *I Can't Be Satisfied*
Track 5: Plays first and second phrases of *I Can't Be Satisfied*
Track 6: Teaching of third phrase of *I Can't Be Satisfied*
Track 7: Plays first three phrases of *I Can't Be Satisfied*
Track 8: Teaching of fourth phrase of *I Can't Be Satisfied*
Track 9: Teaching of fifth phrase of *I Can't Be Satisfied*
Track 10: Teaching of sixth phrase of *I Can't Be Satisfied*
Track 11: Teaching of last phrase of *I Can't Be Satisfied*
Track 12: Plays slowly *I Can't Be Satisfied*
Track 13: Plays up to tempo *I Can't Be Satisfied*
Track 14: Sleepy John Este's recording of *Someday Baby Blues*
Track 15: Jo Ann Kelly and Stefan perform *Someday Baby*
Track 16: Plays *Someday Baby*
Track 17: Teaching of last two phrases of *Someday Baby*
Track 18: Plays last two phrases of *Someday Baby*
Track 19: Teaching of first phrase of *Someday Baby*
Track 20: Teaching of second phrase of *Someday Baby*
Track 21: Plays first and second phrases of *Someday Baby*

Track 22: Teaching of third phrase of *Someday Baby*
Track 23: Plays first three phrases of *Someday Baby*
Track 24: Teaching of fourth phrase of *Someday Baby*
Track 25: Plays first four phrases of *Someday Baby*
Track 26: Teaching of fifth phrase of *Someday Baby*
Track 27: Teaching of sixth phrase of *Someday Baby*
Track 28: Plays *Someday Baby*
Track 29: Fred McDowell plays *Someday Baby*
Track 30: Hambone Willie Newburn's recording of *Roll and Tumble Blues*
Track 31: Plays *Roll and Tumble Blues*
Track 32: Teaching of first two phrases of *Roll and Tumble Blues*
Track 33: Teaching of third phrase of *Roll and Tumble Blues*
Track 34: Teaching of fourth phrase of *Roll and Tumble Blues*
Track 35: Teaching of last phrase of *Roll and Tumble Blues*
Track 36: Plays *Roll and Tumble Blues*
Track 37: Teaching playing the melody line with block chords
Track 38: Muddy Waters' recording of *Roll and Tumble Blues*
Track 39: Baby Face Leroy's recording of *Roll and Tumble Blues*
Track 40: Fred McDowell plays of *Gravel Road Blues*
Track 41: Closing thoughts